RECOGNITION
WITHOUT REWARDS

D0569392

RECOGNITION
WITHOUT REWARDS

CAREN CAMERON

BETTY TATE

DAPHNE MACNAUGHTON

COLLEEN POLITANO

PEGUIS PUBLISHERS
WINNIPEG • CANADA

© 1997 Caren Cameron, Betty Tate, Daphne MacNaughton, and Colleen Politano

All rights reserved. Except as noted, no part of this publication may be reproduced or transmitted in any form or by any means—graphic, electronic, or mechanical—without prior written permission of the publisher. Any request to photocopy any part of this book, other than pages where permission to reproduce is stated, shall be directed in writing to the Canadian Reprography Collective, 379 Adelaide Street W., Ste. M1, Toronto ON M5V 1S5

Printed and bound in Canada by Kromar Printing Limited

98 99 00 01 02 5 4 3 2 1

Canadian Cataloguing in Publication Data

Recognition without rewards

(Building connections)

Includes bibliographical references.
ISBN 1-895411-89-0

1. Motivation in education. 2. Rewards and punishments in education.
I. Cameron, Caren, 1949 – II. Series.

LB1065.R43 1997 370.154 C97-920158-6

Project editing: Annalee Greenberg
Cover photographs: Leon Politano, Colleen Politano

Peguis Publishers
100–318 McDermot Avenue
Winnipeg, Manitoba
Canada R3A 0A2
1-800-667-9673

"With a little help from our friends . . ."

—*Lennon/McCartney*

As we worked on this book, our friends listened, challenged, persisted in endless conversations, and struggled with us. With thanks, we dedicate this book to them.

CONTENTS

ACKNOWLEDGMENTS

We are most appreciative of the many people who have influenced and informed us. In particular, Alfie Kohn has inspired us—whenever we were stuck, we went back to his work and inevitably there was something there to help us work toward schools where students are no longer "punished by rewards."

Moving From Rewards to Recognition

Our Struggle

The seed for this book was planted fifteen years ago, when we, friends and colleagues, started to share our thoughts about rewards. As teachers we had tried using rewards to manage behavior and motivate learning. As parents we had seen the negative effects of rewards on our own children. We had come to realize that rewards had negative effects not only on students who didn't receive them, but on those who did. We intuitively knew that rewards did not work.

As we continued to work with children, parents, and colleagues, we talked about rewards, the prevailing beliefs about their value, and our own changing perceptions about them. We read relevant information and research. We searched for more satisfying and successful ways to work with our students. Today we appreciate the complexity of the issue, and although we do not know all of the answers, we do have a thorough understanding and knowledge of the research and our own experiences.

We have written this book to encourage others to talk and read about the effects of rewards, to questions themselves and others, and to try some of the alternate practices that have worked for us and our students. Our long-term goal is for students to develop the internal desire and skills to be lifelong learners.

This book provides practical ideas and examples of

- ☛ classroom activities that show children ways to recognize and appreciate their own accomplishments and the efforts and successes of others
- ☛ school-wide practices that value the uniqueness of each person and his or her contribution to the school community
- ☛ sports and physical activities that emphasize choice and include cooperative and competitive options
- ☛ year-end events that publicly recognize and celebrate the learning of all students
- ☛ assessment practices that involve students in criteria setting, self-assessment, and goal setting

What do we mean by rewards?

Rewards can be defined as "return or recompense for service or merit, requital (payment) for good or evil." The types of rewards that are offered in schools include everything from praise and stickers, to honor rolls and letter grades. Rewards are contingent on students meeting conditions set by a person in authority.

Our experiences using rewards

When we did our teacher preparation, we learned to manage behavior and motivate learners by using rewards. Looking back at our early years of teaching, we each recall specific incidents that made us stop and question the effects of rewards.

THE READING INCENTIVE PROGRAM at Colleen's school offered prizes to students for the total number of books they read. Colleen overheard Kate (one of her successful readers) in the library, telling her friend that she wanted to find an easy book with lots of pictures (not one Kate *really* wanted to read) so she could get a prize.

This system of rewards was not working. The prize was getting in the way of the very thing that Colleen wanted to promote— Kate's love of reading.

CAREN GAVE EACH ROW OF STUDENTS points for good behavior and erased points when they were not behaving in the way she wanted. On Friday, the rows of students who had accumulated twenty points got to watch a video. Kevin, who never seemed to get ready on time, was getting dirty looks and demands to hurry up from the others in his row. As Caren started to erase a point because Kevin was not ready, he yelled, "I don't want to see that stupid video anyway. My mom got it for me last night and it's dumb!"

This system of rewards was not working. Kevin's behavior didn't change, and he was being rejected by his peers.

E ACH CHILD HAD A STAR CHART posted on the wall. At the end
of the week, students would get a sticker if they had
improved. After a certain number of improvements, Daphne
would give them an additional prize. Once the system was in
place for a month or so, Teresa came up to Daphne and said,
"You know, the gooder I am, the harder this gets."

This system of rewards was not working. Teresa figured out the
system and, following her observation, let her work slide.

I T WAS THE END OF THE YEAR. The principal asked Caren to
choose the top girl and boy from her class for the year-end
awards for achievement, effort, citizenship, and improvement.
Caren knew a number of students would feel betrayed that they
didn't receive trophies, even though she had recognized them
throughout the year. And she knew some parents would question her decisions, no matter what they turned out to be. She
wasn't even clear what she was to be basing her decisions upon.
Caren dreaded this time of year and hated being asked to participate in a process she didn't believe in.

This system of rewards was not working. Caren felt she was
compromising her personal beliefs and the relationships with
her students and their parents.

What we learned

We had tried using rewards. When one reward system didn't
work, we created new and improved ones. Our experiences led
us to the same conclusions:

- ☛ Rewards seemed to manage some behavior, but only for
  brief periods of time. When we stopped giving the
  rewards, the behavior we were trying to change still
  occurred.
- ☛ Rewards needed to be bigger and better to get students to
  "buy in." Students continued to up the ante: "What kind of
  pizza will we get? Will there be pop, too?"
- ☛ Rewards encouraged students to take the easy way out
  and discouraged risk taking.

- Rewards, such as stickers or prizes, became the sole focus; the significance of learning was often lost.

- Rewards put high-achieving students under great pressure to repeat their performance of previous terms and years.

- Rewards discouraged the nonwinners from giving their best effort because they knew that someone else would get the reward.

- Rewards created situations in which students were competing against each other rather than working together.

- Rewards set up situations where students in the same classroom or age group ended up in competitions that were unfair, given their differing developmental levels, interests, strengths, and talents.

- Rewards weren't needed to motivate students. When students were given work they were interested in and able to do, they were motivated.

What the research says

During the time we were asking ourselves questions about rewards and competition, research and informed opinions seemed to converge. Following are some highlights of the research and literature:

- Rewards divert attention from the actual performance and learning, discourage risk taking, and can (when withheld) serve as a form of punishment. Students who are extrinsically motivated tend to select tasks that are low in degree of difficulty (Kohn 1993a, 1993b, 1991; Lepper 1988; Schaps and Lewis 1991).

- Intrinsically motivated students, students who engage in an activity ". . . for its own sake, for the enjoyment it provides, the learning it permits, or the feelings of accomplishment it evokes . . . " (Lepper 1988, 289–309) tend to select tasks that are moderately challenging. When teachers focus on the performance and learning, students are encouraged to take risks and establish further challenges (Kohn 1993a, 1991).

- Rewards undermine interest and motivation (Amabile 1989; Caine and Caine 1994; Deci 1978; Lepper 1988; Lepper and Cordova 1992).

- Teachers can foster interest and creativity by providing quality feedback, which in turn, contributes to intrinsic motivation (Amabile 1989; Goleman et al. 1992; Lepper and Cordova 1992; Lumsden 1994).

- Rewarded behaviors are often short-lived: when the rewards cease, the behavior stops, too (Kohn 1993b; Jensen 1994; Sweet and Guthrie 1996).

- The likelihood of long-term growth, development, learning, and creativity is increased when the learning experience contributes to learners' autonomy rather than to their dependence (Amabile 1989; Caine and Caine 1994; Deci and Ryan 1985; Deci et al. 1991; Sweet and Guthrie 1996).

- Rewards can have negative effects on the self-esteem of winners and losers. Just as there is grave danger for children who experience repeated failure, rejection, and alienation, the student who believes he or she is worthy only through proof of superiority over others is also at risk (Deci 1978; Elkind 1987; Kohn 1986a, 1993a; Orlick and Mosher 1978).

- Students' self-esteem can be enhanced and their self-concept can become more realistic when they are provided with quality feedback (Jensen 1995; Rosenthal and Babad 1985).

- Rewards do not contribute to ideal learning environments (Caine and Caine 1994; Glasser 1986; Greig et al. 1989; Kohn 1986a, 1991, 1993a).

- Optimal learning environments are characterized by physical and emotional safety, positive social bonding, states of high challenge and low stress, control over one's own learning, and the possibility of hope (Borba 1994; Caine and Caine 1994; Jensen 1995).

- "Rewards rupture relationships" (Kohn 1993a, 136).

- When genuinely acknowledged for their efforts and achievements, students develop socially healthy behavior. In optimal learning environments, students feel they belong, and that they are valued and respected; they are friendlier to others and become more respectful and caring toward their peers (Kohn 1993a, 1991; Lumsden 1994).

- Rewards, "because they are predictable *and* have a market value," are a form of bribery. "The primary point . . . is that you don't have to bribe learners to learn. The human brain loves to learn!" (Jensen 1995, 273).

☛ Rewards are extrinsic motivators: students perform a task in order to obtain a reward or avoid punishment (Kohn 1993a, 1993b; Lepper 1988).

☛ Some assessment, evaluation, and reporting practices (including emphasis on grading and the use of letter grades) do not support learning. Such practices interfere with learning because they are artificial, imprecise, and focus on extrinsic rewards rather than the intrinsic value of learning for its own sake (Deci 1978; Kohn 1993a; Smith 1986).

WHERE TO FROM HERE?

The research confirmed what we had learned. Rewards can hinder students from developing positive self-esteem, working successfully with others, taking risks, and accepting responsibility. Above all rewards interfere with learning. To support learners, we need to move away from using rewards systems in our classrooms and schools.

Moving away from rewards

This book is about moving away from practices where teachers give rewards—such as prizes, trophies, extra time in the gym, class and group points, stickers, money, praise, tokens, and grades—to individuals or groups in an attempt to manage behavior and motivate learning. It is about leaving behind practices that are based on conditions adults set for students, where students are told, "If you do this, you'll get this." The book is about leaving behind reward systems because they *interfere with learning*.

When we started to move away from using rewards, however, we faced many questions:

No rewards? Does that mean a student will do well and I'll just have to ignore it because I can't reward him or her?

Can't I ever say anything nice to children again?

What about providing feedback so students can see what they are doing right?

What do we mean by learning?

When we were in school, learning usually meant memorizing. When we refer to learning in this book, we mean thinking, problem solving, constructing, transforming, investigating, creating, analyzing, making choices, organizing, deciding, explaining, talking and communicating, sharing, representing, predicting, interpreting, assessing, reflecting, taking responsibility, exploring, asking and answering, recording, predicting, gaining new knowledge and applying that knowledge to different situations.

Can we still have competitive teams at our school? For some kids team sports are the best part of school.

Don't people deserve to be recognized for special efforts and accomplishments?

If students aren't acknowledged for the good things they do, how can we expect them to continue to work hard?

We wrestled with these concerns and questions. We knew that if we stopped using rewards, we did not want to lose the concept of recognition. We knew students, like all others, needed to be acknowledged for whom they are and what they achieve. We began to develop alternate practices based on research about learning and rewards. This provided us with a direction to follow in our classrooms and schools that would acknowledge students and support their learning. We knew that we needed to understand and plan opportunities for recognition.

What do we mean by recognition?

The word *recognition*, based on the Latin root *cognoscere*, "to know," is defined as "to notice." *Validate, acknowledge, honor,* and *support* are all synonyms. Recognition might include

- ☛ partners giving each other specific feedback on a project
- ☛ students presenting important memories of their year at a year-end celebration
- ☛ a student keeping a personal record of the books he or she read during the term
- ☛ a teacher providing specific feedback on a student's project

The ideas and activities in this book provide specific examples of how recognition can look in classrooms and schools. They show how students work with teachers to develop an ability to recognize themselves and others.

Our criteria for recognition

The words *reward* and *recognition* are often used interchangeably when, by definition, they are very different. To help clarify the meaning of recognition, for ourselves and others, we developed the following criteria. Recognition is:

- ☛ authentic
- ☛ personal
- ☛ inclusive
- ☛ varied

The chart below compares rewards and recognition.

RECOGNITION IS:	REWARDS ARE:
Authentic: based on genuine accomplishments that occur every day	**Artificial:** based on special events or activities set by others
Personal: based on participation and choices of students	**Impersonal:** based on the decisions and choices of others
Inclusive: available to all students without condition	**Exclusive:** available to a select number of individuals who meet conditions set by others
Varied: provides infinite opportunities for recognizing students' successes	**Limited:** restricts opportunities to a finite number of categories

From Building Connections: *Recognition Without Rewards* by Cameron/Tate/MacNaughton/Politano © 1997. May be reproduced for classroom use.

Sometimes we slipped back into giving rewards but the criteria made us aware of what we were doing. Kohn (1993a) expressed what we experienced when he said "we are marinated in a reward system."

The most important distinction between rewards and recognition is that rewards are based on conditions set by others to control behavior and motivate learners. Recognition, on the other hand, involves noticing, validating, describing, or acknowledging learning that is already taking place.

Once we worked with our criteria for recognition, it became clear that meeting some while leaving out others led us to inadvertently create situations that could be as coercive as the reward systems we were moving away from, or did not support the learning of all students.

For example, giving certificates to all students meets the criteria of inclusiveness. However, without offering students personal choices (for example, what they are recognized for and who recognizes them), the certificate may hold little or no meaning. If a certificate is not personally meaningful for a child, it does not meet our criteria for recognition.

Where this is leading

Recognition supports learning. It leads to a sense of belonging, personal power, and an intrinsic motivation to learn.

When students are recognized, they feel they belong to a community of learners. They come to believe, "I know I am important. I know I am cared for. I know I am believed in and trusted to learn. I know when I have made progress. I know when I have reached my goal. I know what I can do. I know what I need to work on. I know I have a place in this classroom and this school. I know I am noticed. I know that I belong."

When students are recognized by themselves and others, they develop personal power. They learn they have choices and understand that, with choice, comes responsibility—to themselves and others.

When students are recognized by themselves and others, they gain confidence, feel supported and encouraged, take risks, and develop a realistic sense of their strengths and possibilities. They become internally motivated.

We believe that, in the long term, recognition for all students helps them develop the internal desire and skills to be lifelong learners.

The next five chapters describe alternatives to rewards—alternatives that recognize all learners. These provide ways to expand opportunities for recognition in classrooms and schools. Suggestions and reactions from our students have helped us refine and improve the ideas. The process is ongoing.

These are ideas we have collected over many years. Pick and choose one or two ideas. We've learned it is impossible to change everything at once.

CLASSROOM IDEAS

MOVING FORWARD

Once we realized that rewards interfered with learning, we started to change some of our classroom practices. We moved away from

☞ handing out rewards, such as stickers, tokens, and points, for "good" work to individuals and groups

☞ holding classroom competitions that required all students to participate

☞ giving praise that focused on personal approval or judgment rather than on describing what the student had accomplished

☞ using rewards, such as points and bribes, or withholding privileges to get students to behave in a certain way

MORE OF, MORE OFTEN

Our emphasis is to provide expanded opportunities for all students to be recognized for a wide range of efforts and accomplishments by peers, teachers, themselves, and others. Some of the practices we include more of, more often are

☞ talking with students about the effects of rewards and recognition

☞ talking with students about how they learn

☞ providing time each day for students to reflect on, record, and share their accomplishments and achievements

☞ rephrasing praise to provide specific feedback that describes the students' work, behavior, and effort

☞ helping students set class and personal goals regarding behavior and learning

We learned it was not our job to "bestow" recognition. It was to expand the opportunities for recognition so that students could recognize themselves and their peers.

Classroom Ideas:

Classroom Ideas: RECOGNIZING OURSELVES AND OTHERS

(ages 5 and up)

An area in a classroom where students have the opportunity to recognize and value their efforts and the accomplishments of others expands the possibilities for recognition.

1. Talk with students about the importance of recognizing their successes and efforts and those of others. Ask them what they might like to be recognized for and what they might recognize others for.

2. Suggest setting up a recognition area or center where students make things to recognize classmates and themselves, family members, custodians, older buddies, and others, for specific work, behavior, and effort.

3. Involve students in creating the area. We say: "What could we do to recognize people?" "What materials would you like to see at the recognition area?" "How could we organize the space and the materials?"

4. Provide opportunities for students to work at the recognition area.

> We often incorporated ideas into things we were already doing in our classroom. For example, the recognition area became part of our already existing writing center.

Classroom Ideas: SHARING OUR ACCOMPLISHMENTS

(ages 5 and up)

Special sharing times, when students are invited to talk about or show something they've accomplished, provide them with another way to recognize themselves and each other. Students can focus on a variety of their own successes and receive validation from their classmates.

1. Talk with students about the value of sharing their accomplishments with others. We include a variety of kinds of achievement in the discussion—getting along, being a fast runner, painting well, and being good at math—to emphasize that the accomplishments are of equal value.

2. Set aside a time each day for students to work with a partner or in small groups to talk about and show their efforts and accomplishments.

> We kept student sharing quick and simple by limiting the number of students who share or by having students share in pairs or small groups.

Classroom Ideas: **USING SPECIFIC FEEDBACK**

(ages 5 and up)

When teachers respond to students' efforts by describing what they see happening rather than offering an opinion or a judgment (praising), it helps students understand and recognize what they are able to do. When students receive specific feedback, it also helps them focus on learning rather than on pleasing adults.

> **We still respond enthusiastically to what students are doing. The key for us is being genuine and not using praise or feedback to control behavior.**

1. Observe yourself talking to students. We've found it helpful to tape ourselves or have a colleague listen to us and tell us what they've heard. We listened to see if many of our responses fell in the category of opinions or judgments; for example: "I really like it!" "What a good job." "I'm proud of you for doing all of that." "Your picture is beautiful!" "Mrs. Stone [*referring to herself in the third person*] is really impressed with the way everyone is working."

2. Shift from praise to specific feedback by using a few descriptive phrases that feel comfortable. We use such comments as: "Your work is complete and well organized." "Your math questions show careful work and thorough checking." "You have lined up all by yourselves and in the correct places." "I see color and attention to detail in this project."

 Classroom Ideas:
COMING TO AGREEMENT

(ages 5 and up)

One way to create a more effective learning environment is to involve students in making the classroom a place that works for everyone. By doing this, students are recognized for their ideas. As a result, they are more likely to take ownership for their own behavior.

List of students' ideas

1. Ask students to talk about classrooms that are good places to learn. We ask, "What would a classroom need to be like so people could do their best learning?" Make a list of the ideas that students give.

2. Discuss with students what they agree to do that will make the classroom a good place to learn. We say, "If this list describes the classroom that you want, then what are we going to have to agree on to make this happen?" On chart paper, record student responses.

3. Work together to revise the class agreement or promise until it satisfies everyone. This may involve developing a number of drafts and may take a week or more to achieve.

4. Post the class agreement or promise. Take time to refer to it regularly (three to four times a day) to keep it current.

We are careful to record the exact words that students give us during the brainstorming session.

Drafts of class agreement

Classroom Ideas: SETTING CLEAR EXPECTATIONS

(ages 5 and up)

When students have been a part of developing a specific set of expectations, they are more likely to be productive and less likely to need external motivation.

1. Have students refer to the classroom agreement or promise as discussed in the previous activity. As a class, have them choose one item as a goal; for example, "We want our class to be clean and tidy."

2. Ask the class to define the specifics of this expectation. For example, we say: "What does it looks like, sound like, and feel like when we are cleaning up?"

3. Make and post a chart showing the specifics of the expectation.

4. Give students time to talk about how they succeed in following the specifics. Talk about how it helps them achieve their expectation—to make the classroom clean and tidy. Ask them to make suggestions as to how they might improve.

5. Continue to use this process to set expectations for other parts of the promise or issues as they arise.

Defining expectations for clean-up

Classroom Ideas: **INFORMING OTHERS**

(ages 5 and up)

Teachers often write notes for students and their families telling about something special a student has done. When we expand this idea by having students identify their own accomplishments, they become important sources of their own feedback, more children are recognized more often, and families often provide more recognition.

1. Talk with students about the importance of letting their families know about what they are learning. We say: "There are so many things that happen in our classroom that your parents want to know about. I would like to be able to send notes home for everyone, but I can't always do that. You know when you have done something well."

2. Invite students to write a note when they do something they want their families to know about. We make cards or special paper available.

3. Make suggestions to get students started. For example, we say: "You have finished the project you have been working on all week. You might want to write a note or card home."

✦ *Classroom Ideas:* CHOOSING AND SHOWING

(ages 5 and up)

When students have choices about how they represent their thinking, it increases the ways to demonstrate their individual abilities and to be recognized for their strengths.

> ### Different Ways To Show What We Know
>
> - draw
> - write a postcard
> - take a photo
> - talk
> - make a poster
> - bring or make
>   something to show
> - write
> - make a list
> - web
> - map
>
> - a poem
> - paint
> - make a book
> - make a diorama
> - make a puzzle
> - sing
> - take a video
> - design a T-shirt
> - make a tape

Ways to show what we know

1. Ask students to brainstorm the different ways that people can show what they know. Make a list of their ideas, post it in the room, and add to it during the year.

2. Pick a time each week for "choosing and showing." Begin by having students share an experience together, such as listening to a reading of a book or a poem, watching a video, or going on a field trip.

3. Have students choose how they will show what they learned about the experience. Then have them plan and complete some form of representation. For example, after a field trip to see salmon, some students wrote a journal, others painted, and others wrote a poem.

4. Give students time to share their work with others.

5. Discuss with students the different ways of representing their learning. Ask what worked for them, what didn't work, and what they would do next time.

CONVERSATION PIECES

The following conversation pieces reflect some of the issues that we have discussed with parents, educators, and students as we moved away from using rewards. We've included them to encourage you to have conversations with others.

Should there be any competition in classrooms? (colleague)

There are different sources of competition in classrooms. Some students choose to compete with themselves or others. Teachers who use reward systems in an attempt to manage behavior and motivate learning, however, create artificial competitions in classrooms. Students come into our classrooms from different backgrounds, at different stages of development, and with different ways of learning. Using rewards, in which all students are required to participate in classroom-wide competitions, is unfair. This type of competition does not support learning.

Doesn't my child deserve to be rewarded when she does well? (parent)

Children deserve to be recognized for doing well. Specific recognition, without conditions and from a variety of sources, supports learning. When students are rewarded, the reward rather than the accomplishment can become the focus.

My students like getting stickers. Can't I give them anymore? (teacher)

Yes, many students do enjoy stickers. The trouble with stickers is that they are usually given to children when they have met the conditions of the teacher. We want to encourage children to set and monitor their own goals for learning. If you want your students to have stickers, we suggest putting them in the hands of the students and letting them determine how to use them. Once the outside conditions are removed, stickers are no longer rewards.

What do you do with the kids in your room who focus on winning and losing? (colleague)

Teachers cannot control student responses. Students come from different backgrounds and experiences. However, when teachers move away from rewards and toward recognition, they shift the focus away from winning and losing in their classrooms. By engaging students in honest and open conversation about recognition and rewards, they start to think about what they say and do.

When you adapt the ideas in this chapter or create new ones for you and your students *remember . . .*

Recognition is:

- ☛ **authentic:** based on genuine accomplishments that occur every day
- ☛ **personal:** based on participation and choices of students
- ☛ **inclusive:** available to all students without condition
- ☛ **varied:** provides infinite opportunities for recognizing students' successes

SCHOOL-WIDE IDEAS

MOVING FORWARD

Once we realized that using rewards at the school level interfered with valuing the uniqueness of each student and building a school community, we started to change some of our school-wide practices. We moved away from

- ☛ having rewards, such as a principal's list or an honor roll, where select students have their names and accomplishments displayed in the school

- ☛ giving, to some students who meet certain conditions, special cards or tokens that buy prizes or privileges

- ☛ showcasing teacher-created displays, where only the best work and top scores are shown

- ☛ having programs, such as Student of the Month, where a limited number of students are featured

MORE OF, MORE OFTEN

Our focus now is to expand the opportunities for recognizing students' unique and diverse talents inside and outside the school community. Some practices we include more of, more often are

- ☛ showcasing student-created displays where a wide variety of accomplishments are featured

- ☛ increasing opportunities for building a sense of school community

- ☛ expanding the recognition of students' accomplishments outside of school

- ☛ recognizing the diversity of expertise within the school community

School-wide Ideas:

★ School-wide Ideas: CREATING YELLOW PAGES

(ages 5 and up)

One way to recognize students, parents, and teachers is to create a catalog of their unique and diverse expertise. When people have opportunities to use their expertise in real and practical ways, recognition is authentic.

1. Show students a copy of the Yellow Pages from a telephone company, and talk about how people use these to get help. Discuss making Yellow Pages so that others know what skills students have and where help is available in your school.

2. Invite students throughout the school to make advertisements for their skills.

3. Collate the advertisements into a book for school-wide distribution. For example, we have one or more individuals, such as school administrators, parents, or teachers, coordinate this project. They decide on how to publish and distribute the Yellow Pages.

You can extend this project to include the skills of family members and others in the school community.

Yellow Page advertisement

Reproducible master in Appendix

For help with ___computers___
ask for ___Josh in Mrs Waldie's class___

Computer Confusion?
Call for Josh at
school room #6.
I have my own
powerbook and
experience using Word
6.0. I have Internet.
I can give you names of
people I've helped.

School-wide Ideas: **INVITING RESPONSES**

(ages 5 and up)

When all students are invited to display their work in the school, opportunities for recognition are increased. When students choose what goes on display, the recognition is personal and authentic.

Approach #1

1. Talk with students about creating personal bulletin boards throughout the year. We say: "You know best what you like, what you are proud of, and how you want it displayed. Talk with a partner about what you might like to display and ways you would design it."

2. Divide hall and classroom display areas into equal sections so each student or group of students has a space.

3. Work together with the class to develop criteria (see page 57, chapter 6) about what an effective display looks like. Talk about how often displays need to be changed.

4. Provide time for students to organize and display their work.

5. Have students assess their display in relation to the criteria.

Approach #2

1. Talk with students about the importance of receiving specific feedback.

2. Ask students to select some work they would like to have displayed outside their classroom.

Reproducible masters in Appendix

I'd like you to notice:

• the detail took a long time
• I made up the border myself

signed: _Andrea_

Personal reflection card

3. Have each student write a personal reflection to go on the display telling what they want others to know about their work.

To _Andrea_

I know what I liked:

I liked *the brilliant colors*

I liked *the bubble letters that were easy to read*

signed: _Mrs. Patton_

Response card

4. Have response cards available so that people who are looking at the display can provide specific feedback.

We made sure each student received completed feedback cards. We responded to student's work ourselves, and encouraged other staff members, students, and parents to respond.

***School-wide Ideas:* LEARNING BEYOND THE SCHOOL**

(ages 5 and up)

When students are invited to show what they do outside of school, it gives them the chance to demonstrate their skills, talents, and interests. This reinforces the belief that learning is ongoing; it happens inside and outside of school and may take many forms.

1. Have a teacher or administrator demonstrate this idea by discussing and displaying some personal learning he or she did outside of school. For example, one principal presented slides of her summer rock-climbing expedition and showed the equipment she used.

2. Talk with students about some of the things they have learned outside of school.

3. Post a sign-up schedule on the wall. Invite interested students to sign up to make a presentation about their out-of-school learning.

4. Have an adult coordinate student presentations for an audience. This could take the form of an afternoon event for the school, a buddy activity, an evening presentation for parents, or a school Open House.

5. Take a photo of each student with his or her display. Exhibit the photos in a prominent place in the school to demonstrate the diversity among the students.

***School-wide Ideas:* SPOTLIGHTING ACHIEVEMENTS**

(ages 5 and up)

Short and regular assemblies provide opportunities to spotlight students' accomplishments. When students are involved in planning the program and introducing and thanking presenters, the opportunities for recognition are increased and the feeling of community is enhanced.

1. Suggest to colleagues that they organize monthly assemblies in which students have opportunities to show their talents and be recognized. Teachers who are interested set aside time for these assemblies and agree to sponsor one for a particular month.

2. Talk with students about the many different talents people in the school possess. Explain that assemblies are being held to recognize people for their talents.

3. Suggest ideas, such as reading a poem, playing the piano, showing a diorama, demonstrating skateboarding skills, or presenting a Readers Theatre. Have students add to the list.

4. Tell students to contact the sponsor for the month to demonstrate their talent and arrange to be spotlighted at an assembly.

5. Invite family members and other community members to the assemblies. We've found that in a large school it may work best to hold one assembly in the morning for half the classes, and one in the afternoon for the other half.

6. Provide students time in class to write individual or class notes to those who were spotlighted at the assembly.

Class note to student performer

Congratulations, Ken

We saw you at the Spotlight Assembly and would like you to know

—We enjoyed your Readers Theatre.
—We thought it was really funny.
—You talked so we could hear you at the back.

Mrs. Stewart's Grade 4 class

✸ *School-wide Ideas:* BUILDING BUDDY PROGRAMS

(ages 5 and up)

Buddy programs enhance the sense of school community by helping children develop relationships with students of different ages. This provides new opportunities for recognition.

1. Find a teacher who wants to start a buddy program. Decide where to meet, when to meet, and how to set up buddy partners.

2. Talk with the students in each class about how the program works and what the benefits are. We emphasize friendship and learning from one another.

3. Begin with a few simple activities, such as reading stories together, drawing pictures of each other, and making lists of favorite people, places, and things. After a few weeks, ask students to contribute ideas of what they would like to do with their buddies.

4. Suggest simple and quick ways for students to recognize each other. For example, at the end of each buddy session, have students tell each other one thing that was fun and one thing they noticed about their buddy. Or, during the day, when one buddy does something special, have him or her write a card to the other buddy telling about the special something.

CONVERSATION PIECES

The idea that using rewards in schools interferes with building a community raises a number of questions and concerns. Consider some of the issues that are being discussed by educators, parents, and students.

It is a competitive world; students need competition in schools to prepare them for the real world. (parent)

The question for us is not, "Should there be competition in schools?" Rather, "How do we help prepare students for the real world?"

To compete in the real world, students need to be problem solvers, self-directed learners, and collaborative workers who will continue to learn long after they leave school. When teachers establish competitions that all students are required to take part in, it can interfere with the development of these skills and attitudes. The experience of working in a school community, where students take on responsibilities, make decisions, and develop relationships, helps prepare them for life—now and in the future.

If you don't acknowledge academic excellence in the school, you give a message to students that academics are not that important. (teacher)

Academics are important, and we need opportunities to recognize academic learning. Schools can recognize and acknowledge academics without giving out single awards for top academic achievement. Our goal is not to downplay academic achievement but to have schools value a wide variety of student accomplishments. Expanding the opportunities for recognition gives students the message that other types of achievement are also valued.

Our school has competitions, such as a school music festival, a school chess tournament, and a Science Fair. Are these bad for kids? (principal)

No, for some children these events are engaging and provide opportunities for recognition. However, for other students these competitions are uninteresting and create anxiety. Students need to decide what competitions they want to participate in and when to participate. Adults need to allow student choice and not give more status to this type of competitive activity over others.

As you and your colleagues adapt the ideas in this chapter or create new ones for you and your students *remember . . .*

Recognition is:

- ☛ **authentic:** based on genuine accomplishments that occur every day
- ☛ **personal:** based on participation and choices of students
- ☛ **inclusive:** available to all students without condition
- ☛ **varied:** provides infinite opportunities for recognizing students' successes

SPORTS AND GAMES IDEAS

MOVING FORWARD

When we looked at school practices related to sports, it was clear that competitive sports provided enjoyment for some students and were a source of anxiety for others. To ensure genuine choice for all students, we focused on widespread participation, enjoyment, teamwork, and skill development.

We moved away from

- ☞ requiring all students in the school to take part in competitive sports activities
- ☞ requiring all students in a physical education class to perform the same tasks (such as fitness tests) where certain students receive rewards (such as badges) for attaining predetermined standards
- ☞ setting up competitive activities in physical education classes (such as races) in which all students were required to participate

MORE OF, MORE OFTEN

Our focus became providing a wide range of options, both competitive and cooperative. That way, students can choose to participate or not. Practices we include more of, more often are

- ☞ involving students in planning and organizing sports events where the focus is on working together
- ☞ providing a range of activities (competitive and noncompetitive) that appeal to all students
- ☞ emphasizing physical activity, teamwork, skill building, and personal and group successes over winning in all competitive and noncompetitive sports activities
- ☞ involving students, parents, and teachers in self-directed physical activities that focus on enjoyment

Sports and Games Ideas:

🧩 *Sports and Games Ideas:* **CHALLENGING OURSELVES**

(ages 9 and up)

Students can learn to recognize their own skills and abilities by keeping a book of personal records.

1. Bring a copy of the *Guinness Book of World Records* to class. Read students several of the records that individuals hold. Talk with students about the many categories of records and the purpose of keeping records.

2. Discuss the idea of keeping a personal book of records for fitness and sports activities. Have students brainstorm possible events that might be included in a personal record book.

3. Work together to establish criteria (see page 57, chapter 6) for keeping a personal book of records.

4. Have students design the pages for their book, with room for descriptions of the event, dates, personal records they've set, comments, and photos.

Page from personal book of records

__Steven Rose's__ **Book of Records**
      (name)

As of __Nov. 15__ my personal record for
      (date)

__pull-ups on the bar__ is
      (activity)

__15__
(number or description)

witness __Ryan Richards__

record setter __Steven Rose__

A goal I'd like to achieve is

__20__

Reproducible master in Appendix

***Sports and Games Ideas:* SIGNING UP TO COMPETE**

(ages 8 and up)

In the beginning, we didn't expect students to write proposals and organize the events without our help – it was a gradual process.

Organize a series of unique competitive events that take place at lunch hour or after school, in which students can choose to compete. These events give students another way to have fun with others, learn new skills, and show what they do well at. When students are involved in the planning, it provides opportunities for recognizing leadership and organizational abilities.

1. Invite students to attend a meeting to talk about sign-up competitions. We emphasize that participation is optional; each student needs to make an individual decision about taking part.

2. Explain to participating students that they need to get a team together and collect, organize, or make the materials they will need.

3. Post activities on sign-up sheets. We plan unique team activities, such as building and flying gliders, making and racing paper turtles, and constructing bridges. Invite students to sign up to take part.

4. Increase student involvement by having them submit proposals for unique events they would like to have as a sign-up competition.

Proposal Form for Sign-Up Competition

Name of Event: _____Power Boat Races_____

Submitted by: _____Steven T._____ *Dave D.*

_____Mike M._____

Contact person: _____Steven T._____

Proposed Event: Make power boats with balloons for power.
(describe it)   The fastest boat wins.

Equipment/Space Required:
        balloons   boats from home or
        kids pools   the kindergarten has some

Possible Date for Event:
        in May so we can do it outside

Please list three reasons why you think this event would
be successful.

    1.   everyone likes this

    2.   we did it once in science

    3.   not everyone got to make one

Date submitted: _____March 10_____

Reproducible master in Appendix

Proposal form for sign-up competition

Sports and Games Ideas: **EXPANDING SPORTS DAYS**

(ages 5 and up)

Noncompetitive sports days, where everyone participates, provide fun and recognition for all students. The days are designed so students can take part in a variety of recreational activities rather than events that require athletic excellence.

Approach #1

1. Discuss the purpose of a Buddy Sports Day with students in both classes. We emphasize cooperation, participation, and fun.

2. Have a buddy class of older students share the responsibility with teachers for creating and managing a sports day for their younger buddies.

3. Work with both classes and brainstorm a list of possible events.

Brainstorm List

- the parachute game
- frog hop with the blanket and the beach ball
- color me a good sport mural
- filler-up (the buckets and the water)
- turtle race
- bubbles
- build a tower
- balloon and bats
- use the earth ball
- bucket toss
- chalk on the sidewalk
- obstacle course
- bike decorating
- scavenger hunt event
- food stop/bathroom break (everyone gets to have their free drink and a rest at the swings)
- green turtle (the gym mats on the kids' backs)

List of events for Buddy Sports Day

4. Make and post a final list of events.

5. Make and post an organizational chart for older buddies so they know who will be leading the events, what equipment they will need, and where the events will take place. They are responsible for running their events.

Event	Equipment	Space	Student Event Leader
1. green turtle	1 gym mat	goal posts on lower field	Kate
2. Chalk on the sidewalk	bucket of large colored chalk	under covered play area	Kevin
3. Food stop	juice, watermelon, bucket of water, paper towels, garbage can	adventure playground near the washrooms	Paul
4. Earth Ball	one earth ball	lower field grass	Dave
5. Nerf Ball Toss	3 garbage cans, 3 nerf balls	basketball court	Steven
6. Build a tower	recycled plastic containers, blocks, rulers, paper cups	beside main entrance	Rasoul

Organizational chart for Buddy Sports Day

6. Arrange the younger students into groups and assign an older buddy (one who is not responsible for an event) as a leader for each group.

7. Meet with both classes after the Buddy Sports Day to review what worked, what needed to be changed, and what they'd like to add the next time.

8. Provide a second opportunity during the year for students to plan another Buddy Sports Day so they can use what they have learned.

Approach #2

1. Discuss the purpose of a Multi-age Sports Day with all students. We emphasize cooperation, participation, and working as a team. Reassure students who like to compete in traditional track-and-field events that there are options for them to compete at other times, but that this is a co-operative activity.

2. Decide on the age spread of the groups. We have two students from each grade level on each multi-age team.

3. Decide on recreational events that are appropriate for the age range, and assign an adult volunteer to oversee each event. Examples of activities include balloon volleyball, parachute activities, earth-ball soccer, bubble-gum-blowing contests, watermelon-eating races, tower building with cups, and water-carrying relays.

4. Organize and post the multi-age teams. We have teams meet before the sports day to decide on team names, cheers, symbols, colors, and leaders.

5. On Multi-age Sports Day, assign each team to a starting event. The parent who oversees the event provides directions. Teams complete the event and move on. Teams can go to the events in any order. We organize at least one more event than the number of teams we have so that there is always an open event to go to.

6. Have all students in the school meet together when the events are completed. Recognize each team for an outstanding performance. For example "The yellow team built a tower of thirty-nine cups before it tipped over." We take team photos and hear team cheers to recognize each group for its outstanding performance.

✻ Sports and Games Ideas: PRACTICING SKILLS

(ages 5 and up)

When we establish special times for students to choose from a variety of activities in a physical education class, we increase the potential for success and recognition.

Approach #1 *(ages 5 to 8)*

1. Establish a regular Choice Day, when younger students practice an activity or skill that they want to improve.

2. Before Choice Day, brainstorm a list of sports equipment students would like to use to practice their skills.

3. Work together to develop criteria (see page 57, chapter 6) for Choice Day.

Criteria for Choice Day

> ## Criteria
>
> On choice day we will:
>
> · be active
>
> · be safe
>
> · be fair and share

4. On Choice Day, divide the gym into three or four sections. Place different pieces of equipment in each section.

5. Ask students to work in the section of their choice and practice their skills. They may decide to change to a different section during the period.

6. After Choice Day, have students assess their use of Choice Day in relation to the agreed-upon criteria.

Approach #2 *(ages 8 and up)*

1. Plan specific times when older students can practice their skills in competitive or noncompetitive situations.

2. Invite students to choose how they want to practice, and have them sign up on charts.

○   ○

Competitive Game

1. Andrew
2. Lisa
3. Sandy
4. Eric
5. Aaron
6. Dave
7. Mike
8. Stephen
9. Diego
10. _____

*one signature per line
Practice on court #1.

Sign-up charts for practicing basketball skills

○   ○

Individual Practice

1. Mark
2. Kyle
3. Rayota
4. Leon
5. Wayne
6. Sue
7. Alanna
8. Janet
9. _____
10. _____
11. _____
12. _____

*one signature per line
Practice on outdoor court.

3. Have students practice their skills. We meet with the class after practice and discuss their choices, how the process worked for them, and what we'll do next time.

○   ○

Partner Practice

1. Katie + Andrea
2. John L. + Leslie
3. Tammy + Phaedra
4. Billy + Doug
5. _____ + _____

*sign up with partner
Practice on court #2.

✱ Sports and Games Ideas: TEACHING OLD GAMES

(ages 5 and up)

Have teachers or other adults teach a game that is an old favorite, such as jacks, hopscotch, or Seven-up, to another person or group. This increases the possibilities for individuals to work together, be involved, have fun, and be recognized.

1. Talk with colleagues and family members about games they used to play.

2. Have volunteers agree to teach a game to another person or group in the school during recess, lunch, or in a physical education class.

3. Ask each person or group who learns the new game to teach it to another person or group within one week.

4. Post a running record of the games taught, the people who taught them, and the people who learned them.

5. Have a celebration hour where everyone in the school or class can choose to watch or take part.

CONVERSATION PIECES

When we talked about including noncompetitive sports and games in schools, some people felt we were asking for a commitment to one or the other—competitive or noncompetitive. However, in moving away from rewards, our focus is on providing a wide range of competitive and noncompetitive sports options. You might consider what colleagues and parents are thinking and talking about as you move away from using rewards in sports.

Doesn't the possibility of winning push you to do your best?
(teacher)

The challenge of competition, not winning, can push some people to do their best. Many researchers and sports psychologists agree that the brain requires challenge to enhance performance. They also recognize that the anxiety created by the pressure of winning may interfere with performance. We can't assume that the possibility of winning pushes all people to do their best. Our focus has therefore become talking with students about what motivates them to do their best. We also make clear that they have choices: to compete against others, with themselves, or not at all.

Can we still have competitive teams at our school?   (teacher)

Yes, we have competitive teams because they provide an opportunity for some students to be recognized for their skills and talents. We are not saying that all competition is bad. Our emphasis in any competitive activity is on the challenge, the opportunity for success, the chance to belong to a group, and the development of skills, rather than on the reward of winning.

Isn't competition a part of physical education classes?   (parent)

Some students will choose to compete—with themselves and with others—in physical education classes. However, when a teacher sets up competitions that require everyone to participate, the competition is unfair because of the range of differences in physical development and experience found in every group of students. Competition of this kind can interfere with the development of skills and interests.

When you adapt the ideas in this chapter or create new ones for you and your students *remember* . . .

Recognition is:

- ☞ **authentic:** based on genuine accomplishments that occur every day
- ☞ **personal:** based on participation and choices of students
- ☞ **inclusive:** available to all students without condition
- ☞ **varied:** provides infinite opportunities for recognizing students' successes

YEAR-END IDEAS

MOVING FORWARD

We realized that, by giving year-end awards to individuals singled out as "the best" in certain categories, many students were not being recognized at all. Such awards undermined the community-building effects of recognition throughout the year. For this reason, we changed some of our year-end practices. We moved away from

- ☛ giving out awards and trophies that rank individuals, such as, *top academic, best citizen, most improved,* or *number-one athlete*

- ☛ giving all students individual certificates and then handing out additional special awards to a select group of students

- ☛ giving more status to one area over another, such as to academic achievement over fine arts, or to district competitions over school accomplishments

MORE OF, MORE OFTEN

We began to focus on creating and maintaining ceremonies and traditions that recognized the collective and individual successes of all learners. Some of the activities that we include more of, more often are

- ☛ providing opportunities for students and teachers to reflect on the things that have taken place during the year

- ☛ focusing on the learning that has taken place during the year

- ☛ inviting students to participate in the planning and presentation of year-end activities

- ☛ inviting family members to share in the celebration and successes of their children

Year-end Ideas:

Year-end Ideas: **LOOKING BACK AND MOVING FORWARD**

(ages 8 and up)

We recognize students who are moving to another school at the end of the year by providing them with an opportunity to reflect on their experiences. This also shows students that each one of them is special.

Approach #1

1. Talk with students about the experiences they have had at the school. Ask students to work with a partner or in a small group and talk about some of the things they remember about school from the time they started kindergarten (or whenever they entered the school) until now. Have each student complete a form telling what they would like to be remembered for and what they are looking forward to.

2. Ask students to bring two photographs—one of when they were young and one that is current. The photographs provide a visual reminder of the student's uniqueness and growth over time.

3. Make one transparency (colored, if possible) of the photos side by side.

4. Plan time for students to rehearse in class. They practice showing the transparencies and reading the comments they've written.

5. Have students make their presentations at a year-end ceremony.

> **Creating new traditions at end-of-year ceremonies required a lot of discussion with students, teachers, and parents before we made any changes!**

What students would like to be remembered for

I would like to be remembered for...

helping out in the kindergarten and looking after the pets in the library

I'm looking forward to...

having a whole bunch of different teachers

signed: _____Sheena_____

Reproducible master in Appendix

Approach #2

1. Talk with students about the importance of taking time to reflect on, remember, and publicly celebrate the highlights of their years at the school.

2. Ask students to complete a form on which they tell about a special memory.

Reproducible master in Appendix

> **A special memory for me is:**
>
> when we had the sleepover in
> the gym when I was in kindergarten.
>
> **I'd like** _Mrs. Anderson_ **to tell something he or she remembers about me.**
>
> **signed:** _Natasha_

Student's special memory

3. Each student then nominates someone—a classmate, teacher, or friend—to tell something special about him or her.

4. Have students invite the person they've nominated to speak about them at the assembly. Each student needs to give the speaker a copy of the form with his or her special memory. We keep our own list of who will be speaking about each student.

5. Purchase a special memento, such as a medallion, individual plaque, or special photo certificate, for each student.

6. Have the nominated person read the student's favorite memory, tell a personal remembrance, and present the memento at a year-end classroom ceremony.

We used funds previously allocated for purchasing trophies, plaques, and prizes that went to a few students and bought mementos for each student leaving the school.

***Year-end Ideas:* LOOKING AT LEARNING**

(ages 5 and up)

A powerful way to recognize all students for their authentic achievements and accomplishments is to have a slide show at the end of the school year. When the audience sees the learning that took place throughout the year, it reminds them that there is much to celebrate in classrooms and schools.

1. Take pictures of everyday events throughout the year, such as students working on a science experiment, having fun on the adventure playground, working with buddies, or high jumping at the District Track Meet.

2. Have at least two to three slides of each student in your class. We use a class list so no one is forgotten.

3. Select a piece of music to play when the slides are being shown. Divide the length of the piece of music by the number of seconds you want to show each slide. Select the appropriate number of slides for the length of the music (we find anything less than five seconds per slide too short).

4. Check the slide show by listening to the music and watching to see if the music and the pictures match. When you have an order that works, number the slides.

5. Show the students a preview of the slide show in class so they can talk about it, laugh about it, and share their comments before it is shown to a larger audience.

6. Show the slides to an audience of parents, family members, or peers at a year-end celebration in the class or with the whole school.

This activity also works with video, colored transparencies, or multimedia presentations.

✦ Year-end Ideas: REMEMBERING THE GOOD TIMES

(ages 5 and up)

We take time at the end of the year to have students reflect on what was personally meaningful during the year. This allows students to appreciate what they have achieved and reflect on their experiences as a group.

Approach #1

1. As the end of the year approaches, talk with students about the importance of remembering the things they've enjoyed doing together.

2. Ask students what they would like to have one more opportunity to do during the last week of school. This might include such things as using the parachute in the gym, finger painting, singing a song from the Christmas concert, or seeing a favorite video.

3. Work together to create a list of favorite activities.

4. Make time to do these favorite activities again and reminisce about them.

What do you want to do
one more time?

- eat lunch together

- get the parachute and use it again

- play math wizards

- go back to the beach and make plaster of paris fish

- have a games afternoon (where we go around and do different games all afternoon)

- meet with our buddies to paint outside

- use the computer lab all morning again with Mr. King

List of activities to do one more time

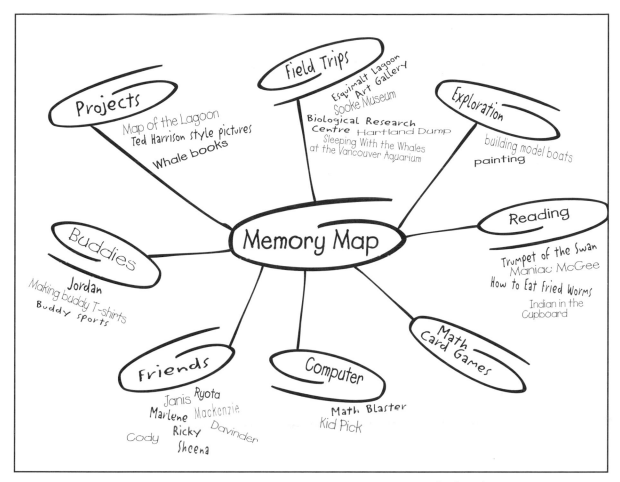

Students' memory map

Approach #2

1. Reflect on some of the year's events by using a mind-mapping technique. Have groups of three to four students map their memories of the year onto large pieces of paper that are posted around the room.

2. Have groups walk around the room to see what other groups have written.

3. Have each student map his or her memories of the year. We encourage students to use the ideas around the room to prompt their thinking.

4. Bring students together. Have each student share one favorite memory. Encourage students to share individual mind maps with others, such as family, friends, or buddies.

This activity worked well when we used it as a last buddy meeting of the year.

Year-end Ideas: **CELEBRATING THE YEAR TOGETHER**

(ages 5 to 8)

When students and family members get together at the end of the school year, it helps everyone appreciate the special time that the class spent together.

> **We keep the celebration short – a maximum of one-and-a-half hours.**

1. Talk with students about sharing accomplishments. Suggest the idea of sharing their thoughts with family members and friends.

2. Schedule an evening in the classroom for celebrating the year together. Make invitations for students to take home.

3. Ask students to tell a partner one thing they did during the year that they are proud of.

4. Give each student a transparency and pens. Ask them to draw a picture of what they are proud of and write a statement telling about it.

5. Provide time for students to rehearse their presentation, practicing their statement and using the overhead projector.

6. Begin the year-end celebration with a brief introduction. Then have students step forward, display their drawings on the overhead, and tell about the one thing they are proud of.

7. End the celebration with students and guests sharing the snacks they have brought.

Invitation for celebrating the year

> **Please Join Us to Celebrate Our Year**
>
> Time: 6:45 - 8:00
> Place: Classroom 7 and library
>
> Program:
> 6:45   Put your snack in the classroom
> 7:00   Go to library to hear memories
> 7:30   Move to classroom to look at the work we've collected and enjoy snacks
>
> Please bring a simple snack to share and whatever your family would like to drink. We'll have cups and napkins ready.

🧩 *Year-end Ideas:* SHARING THE STAGE

(ages 5 and up)

When students share the role of planning for and presenting at a year-end ceremony, the event can become more meaningful for everyone. It provides an opportunity for all students to be on the stage and present their reflections.

Approach #1

1. Talk with students about planning for and presenting at the year-end ceremony.

2. Give students a planning frame and ask them to complete it.

3. As teacher, complete the same frame, one for each student.

Planning frames for reflection

> **You may know that** I love to draw and I draw on everything (even my notebooks)
>
> **But did you know that** Mr. Belcher framed one of my pictures and has it hanging in his office?
>
> signed: ___Mike___

> **You may know that** Michael is good at sports and looked after the sign-out of equipment all year long
>
> **But did you know that** he is writing his own book and illustrating it?
>
> signed: ___Mrs. Lane___

4. Set up a short rehearsal time with each student. Share your completed frames with each other, so the student knows what the teacher is going to say and the teacher knows what the student is going to say.

5. At the year-end ceremony, have each student and his or her teacher stand together and read what they have written.

Reproducible masters in Appendix

Approach #2

1. Talk with students about some of the things that are important about the class. For example, we develop lists of ideas describing how we've worked together, the things we've done, the things we've learned, and the ways we're unique.

Example of a collaborative poem

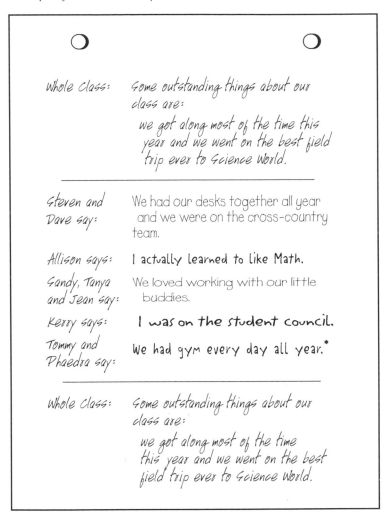

Whole Class:	Some outstanding things about our class are: we got along most of the time this year and we went on the best field trip ever to Science World.
Steven and Dave say:	We had our desks together all year and we were on the cross-country team.
Allison says:	I actually learned to like Math.
Sandy, Tanya and Jean say:	We loved working with our little buddies.
Kerry says:	I was on the student council.
Tommy and Phaedra say:	We had gym every day all year.*
Whole Class:	Some outstanding things about our class are: we got along most of the time this year and we went on the best field trip ever to Science World.

* The poem continues until every student has spoken.

2. Suggest writing a collaborative poem for a year-end presentation.

3. As a class, develop the opening and closing lines of the poem.

4. Then have students, either individually or with partners, write a statement about what was outstanding for them.

5. Have everyone share their statements and assemble them into a class poem.

6. Present the poem at a year-end ceremony. The class reads the opening and closing lines together. The individuals or partners read the lines they wrote until everyone in the class has had a turn.

CONVERSATION PIECES

It is a challenge to make changes to year-end traditions. We found it important to discuss the issues surrounding year-end ceremonies—such as awards, trophies, and other honors—with everyone affected, including parents, students, teachers, and administrators.

If kids don't get awards at the end of the year, why would they do their best? We will end up with a mediocre society. (parent)

Moving away from reward systems does not mean moving away from excellence. The assumption that giving awards at the end of the year motivates all students, both those who receive awards and those who don't, is incorrect. In fact, the opposite can be true. Rewards can interfere with people taking risks and doing their best learning. Research shows that students who receive rewards tend to select tasks that are low in degree of difficulty in order to get the reward. Further research shows that the best learning takes place in classrooms where students are intrinsically motivated and encouraged to take risks.

The year-end awards ceremony is a big occasion at our school. Why should we stop? (teacher)

We do not think that year-end ceremonies need to be stopped. More than that, we believe that traditions are essential to school communities. We do think that if all students are recognized for their accomplishments, the focus shifts to celebrating learning, being valued, and belonging to the communities of classroom and school.

Parents like it when their child wins a trophy. They take it home and put it on the mantel. (teacher)

Everyone wants to see children succeed. However, succeeding and winning are different things. A trophy is a symbol of winning that may, in the long run, interfere with a child's success by putting pressure on the individual to repeat the performance. Expanding opportunities for recognition makes it possible for all students and their families to celebrate successes.

If you don't give out trophies anymore, what happens to all the trophies that have been donated to the school?   (administrator)

Trophies are a part of the history of the school. Teachers, families, and students need to be involved in discussions about what to do with the trophies. One idea is to display the trophies in a cabinet, along with old reading textbooks, the school bell, and other school artifacts or memorabilia.

We include all of our students by giving everyone certificates, and yet we also give out the trophies at the end of the year. Is this a problem?   (principal)

This is a problem because most students will see the trophies as the real awards. The practice of giving trophies still puts all students into competition without giving them a say in whether they wish to be participants. The emphasis on celebration, recognizing accomplishments of all students, and feeling of community are negated by giving trophies to a limited number of people.

When you adapt the ideas in this chapter or create new ones for the year-end ceremonies for your school *remember . . .*

Recognition is:
- ☞ **authentic:** based on genuine accomplishments that occur every day
- ☞ **personal:** based on participation and choices of students
- ☞ **inclusive:** available to all students without condition
- ☞ **varied:** provides infinite opportunities for recognizing students' successes

Assessment Ideas

MOVING FORWARD

Once we realized that ranking, comparing one student to another, and letter grades were reward systems that did not support the learning of all students, we began to change some of our assessment and evaluation practices. We moved away from

- ☞ putting students' scores, marks, or letter grades on public display by, for example, posting marked work, spelling charts, or math drill scores
- ☞ using words that compare and label students, such as *excellent, average, above average, middle of the class, top performance*
- ☞ carrying out all assessment without involving students in the process

MORE OF, MORE OFTEN

Our focus became the importance of self-assessment, setting personal goals, developing criteria with students, and evaluating student performance in relation to criteria—not other students. The activities we include more of, more often are

- ☞ providing more opportunities for specific feedback
- ☞ involving students in assessment practices that show growth over time
- ☞ giving students opportunities to demonstrate their learning in a variety of ways and on an ongoing basis
- ☞ involving students in developing criteria to help them understand what a mark or score stands for
- ☞ assessing student work in relation to criteria rather than in relation to other students

Assessment Ideas:

✸ *Assessment Ideas:* USING CRITERIA

(ages 8 and up)

Setting criteria with students lets them know what counts in their work. Criteria help students recognize what they are good at, what they need to improve, and what they are working toward. When students assess their work in relation to the criteria, they can focus on their learning rather than on a number or grade.

1. Talk with students about what criteria are and why using criteria supports learning. We define criteria as "what counts."

2. Start developing criteria with students by asking a question about a familiar topic. We ask, "What makes a good friend?"

3. Brainstorm responses to the question and list them, using the students' own words.

4. Sort and categorize the ideas on the list into three to five criteria.

5. Use the same process, replacing the example with something students are doing in class; for example, "What makes an effective oral report?"

6. Use the same process to develop criteria for any topic, behavior, or assignment. We have found that it is important to add to and change the criteria over time.

Brainstorm and categorize to develop criteria

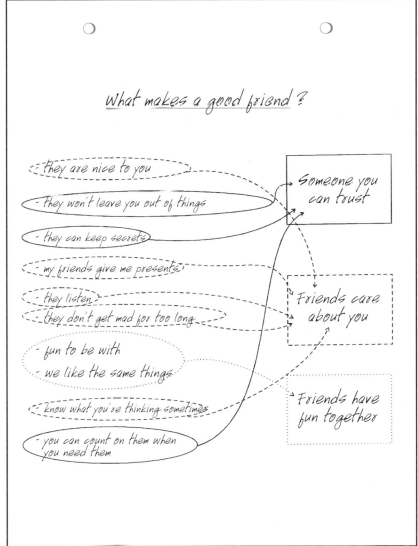

From: *Setting and Using Criteria.* Used by permission, Connections Publishing

Assessment Ideas: **SETTING PERSONAL GOALS**

(ages 5 and up)

When students set personal goals, they have a chance to recognize and celebrate their achievements, and to develop skills that will be valuable throughout their lives.

1. Begin a discussion with students on goal setting. We ask: "Why do people set goals? Whom do you know who sets goals?"

2. Show students how to set goals by emphasizing the importance of working on specific, achievable steps.

3. Use the goal-setting steps shown at left to model a personal goal for your students.

4. Ask students to use the process by setting a goal for the day.

5. Provide students with time during the day to review their goal—to talk about it, ask questions, and celebrate their progress.

6. Repeat the process. Remind students to use the steps for personal goal setting regularly throughout the year.

> Picture: What do you want to be able to do?
>
> Part: What specific part of the goal will you start with?
>
> Plan: How will you get there? How long will it take?
>
> Partner: Who will support you and keep you moving forward?
>
> Party: How will you celebrate achieving your goal?

Goal-setting steps

We found that having a frame to follow is sometimes helpful when students are trying something for the first time. Later on, students adapt it to suit their own needs.

Assessment Ideas: KEEPING PERSONAL RECORDS

(ages 8 and up)

By developing personal records, students focus on their own growth over time and see how much they have accomplished. Personal records consist of lists, scores, times, or other information that students collect to monitor their own learning, in much the same way as a swimmer keeps track of his or her own swim times.

1. Tell students they are going to keep personal records. Talk about how keeping track of work and seeing growth over time is important to learning.

Student example of a calendar record

Record of ___the books I read this month.___

September

		Bridge to 1 Terabithia (Katherine Patterson)	2	3	4	5
6	Dicey's 7 Song (Cynthia Voight)	8	9	Julie of 10 the Wolves (Jean George)	11	12
13	14 Kids Consumer Report magazine p. 17-21	15	The 16 Egypt Game (Z. Snyder)	17	18	19
20	21	22	23 Fire's Burning (J. Lawson)	Kids 24 World 10 pages	25	26
27	28	29	30			

Notice that: ___I like fiction best. I don't have a total number of pages but it is about 600.___

What's Next: ___I'd like to try to get some other books by Julie Lawson.___

Reproducible master in Appendix

2. Work together to develop a list of things that people might keep personal records for. This might include books a student has read, words a student knows how to spell, titles of stories a student has written, or the different ways the student has represented his or her learning.

3. Begin by having students each keep a personal record of the same type. For example, we have students keep a personal record of the books they have read during a month.

4. Give each student a blank copy of a calendar (or any other form that makes record keeping easy) and provide time for students to record their book titles.

5. Use this record to help students set goals. Ask students to look at their personal records and decide what goal they would like to achieve next.

6. Give students the option of sharing their personal records and celebrating their successes with others.

Assessment Ideas: REQUESTING PEER RESPONSE

(ages 6 and up)

When students respond to one another's work, they can build relationships, identify sources of help, and provide one another with genuine, meaningful, and immediate feedback.

Approach #1

1. Talk with students about how people require specific feedback to learn. We ask students to describe what people say and do that helps them learn. For example, they might say, "When you were talking to the class you looked at all of us and we could really hear your voice." "When you were reading I understood the story because you kept changing your voice to make it interesting."

2. Ask students to give another person specific feedback while they are working on a project. We say: "Stop what you are doing right now and take four steps in any direction. Look at the person closest to you, and provide specific feedback on the work that he or she is doing. Then have that person describe your work to you."

3. Bring students together to discuss the feedback they gave to one another. Discuss what was helpful and what wasn't helpful.

Approach #2

1. Ask students to pause while they are working and form groups of three.

2. Explain to students that one of them will be a presenter, one will be an encourager, and one will be an advisor.

3. Tell the students that presenters show their work to the group, encouragers say something positive to the presenter about their work, and advisors give one specific piece of advice.

4. Signal students to return to their individual activities.

5. Repeat the process, having students change roles until everyone has been a presenter, an encourager, and an advisor.

We use the acronym APE to help our students remember their different roles. They call this activity "Going Ape."

✦ *Assessment Ideas:* DEMONSTRATING LEARNING

(ages 6 to 10)

When a students demonstrate their learning about a specific topic for an audience, they have the opportunity to practice skills and receive recognition.

1. Ask students to talk with a partner about what they have learned during the study of a specific theme or unit.

2. Have students brainstorm everything they have learned about the topic the class decided on. Record ideas on a chart.

Lists of what students know, and ways to show others

What We Know About the Brain	Ways to Show
– has 4 lobes	– make playdough brain models to show parts
– 2 sides	– draw and label posters of the brain
– wrinkled	– write brain poems
– squishy like porridge	– create a list of brain math using numbers related to the brain such as 2 sides, 4 lobes and infinite connections
– cerebellum for balance	
– it makes connections	
– mostly made of water	
– different parts do different things	– use objects to illustrate things we knew about the brain such as: a raisin shows the wrinkles, a cabbage shows the size, a walnut shows 2 halves and skull
– skull protects it	
– has a stem	
– everyone has one	

3. Ask students to suggest ways they could show others about what they know. List their suggestions on the chart.

4. Together, determine one way the class can demonstrate its knowledge of the topic. Determine ways individuals or small groups can show their learning.

5. Make a simple plan for a presentation to an audience of family and guests. Our plan includes a group demonstration, such as a Readers Theatre piece, a song or a poem, and individual demonstrations, such as readings or presentations of work.

6. Invite guests to fill out comment cards for both the class and their child after the performance.

We often need to remind family members to provide feedback on comment cards; sometimes we end up doing it ourselves.

 Assessment Ideas: **CREATING PROGRESS FOLIOS**

(ages 5 and up)

Progress folios are a concrete way to help students recognize their progress and to show parents their child's individual growth. The structure of the progress folios provides an at-a-glance picture of learning for students, as well as for family members and teachers.

Progress folio categories

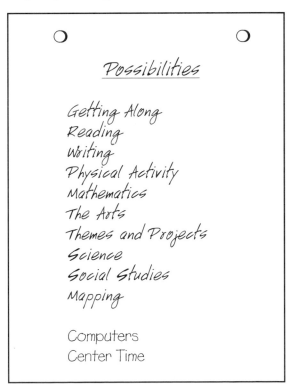

Possibilities

Getting Along
Reading
Writing
Physical Activity
Mathematics
The Arts
Themes and Projects
Science
Social Studies
Mapping

Computers
Center Time

1. Talk with students about how creating a collection of work shows progress over time.

2. Suggest to students some possible categories —areas where they can see progress—and ask if they can think of any others.

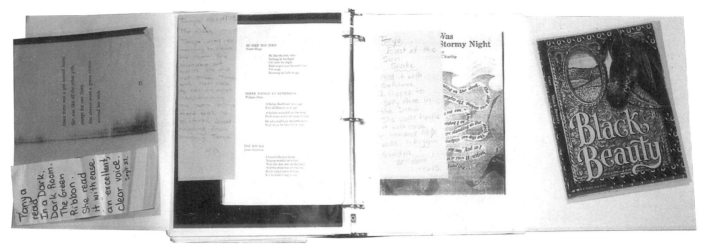

Progress folio

Sample page

3. Decide how to organize and present work samples from the categories you've decided on. We like to use binders with 11" x 17" (280 cm x 432 cm) paper folded in half as the inserts. When open, the page provides four spaces for each category, with one space for each term.

4. Start by having students design a first page and label a section for each category.

5. Provide class time early in the year for students to make or select a work sample for each category and put it into their progress folio.

6. Invite students to show their first samples to family members, a buddy, or to other adults in the school.

7. Set aside time before each reporting period for students to review their entries and to add new samples in each category that show growth and improvement.

8. Have students present the progress folios at reporting conferences or when parents or guests visit the classroom. Students take their progress folios home at various times during the year. Provide a page at the back of the progress folio for responses from people who have looked through it.

> As we started this activity, we reminded ourselves to focus on showing growth over time. We started with five categories. We make a sample progress folio so students can see how they are used.

CONVERSATION PIECES

Most people were not involved in their own assessment when they were in school, but assessment practices are changing. Reading about assessment practices that support learning informed our thinking. Talking with others let us in on their struggles.

I am required to give letter grades. Aren't they just another form of rewards? (teacher)

Yes, letter grades are a system of rewards that we believe interfere with learning. While we continue to make this argument to parents and the public, the reality is that most of us are required to give letter grades on report cards three to four times a year.

What we are not required to do, however, is to put a letter grade or a number (reward) on each piece of work that a student completes. Instead, students receive specific criteria-based feedback from a variety of sources. We use this data to make our judgments and provide letter grades as required.

How will I know how my child is doing? (parent)

If parents want to know how their child is doing, they need to talk with their child and teacher. We're concerned that parents often rely on letter grades to tell them how their child is progressing. Letter grades are imprecise and can give a false sense of how and what a child is learning. Teachers can provide parents with specific information on the expectations for students and criteria for assignments. Parents can view work samples that show evidence of their child's growth. Such conversations offer a wealth of information that go well beyond a letter-grade symbol.

Where do people get the time to assess and recognize all students? (teacher)

We do not see recognition as separate from assessment—when we recognize students with specific feedback, we are assessing their work. It is not added to what teachers are already required to do. In fact, by involving students and peers in the process of recognition, the teacher is not required to do it all and know it all. When we saw how capable our students were of taking on responsibilities, we stopped doing it all ourselves. This applies to both assessment and recognition.

Isn't it the teachers' job to evaluate students?   (parent)

Yes, it is the teachers' job to evaluate students. We are accountable for making judgments about where individual students stand in relation to widely held expectations (provincial or state guidelines). We make a distinction between assessment and evaluation. By assessment, we mean gathering evidence of student learning. By evaluation, we mean interpreting evidence and making judgments based on this data. Because teachers require data to be able to make judgments, students and teachers are both key participants in the data-collection process. When teachers involve students in the process of assessment, they are not giving away their responsibility. Teachers actually become more accountable for their judgments, and students take more responsibility for their work.

When you adapt the ideas in this chapter or create new ones for your students *remember . . .*

Recognition is:

- ☛ **authentic:** based on genuine accomplishments that occur every day
- ☛ **personal:** based on participation and choices of students
- ☛ **inclusive:** available to all students without condition
- ☛ **varied:** provides infinite opportunities for recognizing students' successes

CONCLUSION

KEEPING THE CONVERSATIONS GOING

We have written about our experiences and stories. We wrote this book to encourage others to talk and read about the effects of rewards, to ask questions of themselves and others, and to use and adapt some of our ideas for recognition. We invite you, your friends and colleagues, your students and their families to explore these ideas.

We can't take on the whole world at once – when people come together over time, great things happen.

APPENDIX:
BLACKLINE MASTERS

For help with _____

ask for _____

From Building Connections: *Recognition Without Rewards*, by Caren Cameron, Betty Tate, Daphne MacNaughton, Colleen Politano © 1997. May be reproduced for classroom use.

Yellow Page advertisement

From Building Connections: *Recognition Without Rewards*, by Caren Cameron, Betty Tate, Daphne MacNaughton, Colleen Politano © 1997. May be reproduced for classroom use.

I'd like you to notice:

-

-

signed: _____

I'd like you to notice:

-

-

signed: _____

I'd like you to notice:

-

-

signed: _____

Personal reflection card   71

To _____

I know what I liked:

I liked

I liked

signed: _____

To _____

I know what I liked:

I liked

I liked

signed: _____

To _____

I know what I liked:

I liked

I liked

signed: _____

From Building Connections: *Recognition Without Rewards*, by Caren Cameron, Betty Tate, Daphne MacNaughton, Colleen Politano © 1997. May be reproduced for classroom use.

From Building Connections: *Recognition Without Rewards*, by Caren Cameron, Betty Tate, Daphne MacNaughton, Colleen Politano © 1997. May be reproduced for classroom use.

_____ **Book of Records**
(name)

As of _____ my personal record for
(date)

_____ is
(activity)

_____.
(number or description)

witness _____

record setter _____

A goal I'd like to achieve is

_____.

Proposal Form for Sign-Up Competition

Name of Event: _____

Submitted by: _____ _____

_____

Contact person: _____

Proposed Event:
(describe it)

Equipment/Space Required:

Possible Date for Event:

Please list three reasons why you think this event would be successful.

         1.

         2.

         3.

Date submitted: _____

From Building Connections: *Recognition Without Rewards*, by Caren Cameron, Betty Tate, Daphne MacNaughton, Colleen Politano © 1997. May be reproduced for classroom use.

From Building Connections: Recognition Without Rewards, by Caren Cameron, Betty Tate, Daphne MacNaughton, Colleen Politano © 1997. May be reproduced for classroom use.

I would like to be remembered for…

I'm looking forward to…

signed: _____

I would like to be remembered for…

I'm looking forward to…

signed: _____

I would like to be remembered for…

I'm looking forward to…

signed: _____

A special memory for me is:

I'd like _____ to tell something
he or she remembers about me.

signed: _____

A special memory for me is:

I'd like _____ to tell something
he or she remembers about me.

signed: _____

A special memory for me is:

I'd like _____ to tell something
he or she remembers about me.

signed: _____

From Building Connections: *Recognition Without Rewards*, by Caren Cameron, Betty Tate, Daphne MacNaughton, Colleen Politano © 1997. May be reproduced for classroom use.

From Building Connections: *Recognition Without Rewards*, by Caren Cameron, Betty Tate, Daphne MacNaughton, Colleen Politano © 1997. May be reproduced for classroom use.

You may know that

But did you know that

signed: _____

You may know that

But did you know that

signed: _____

You may know that

But did you know that

signed: _____

Record of _____

Notice that: _____

_____

_____

What's Next: _____

_____

From Building Connections: Recognition *Without Rewards*, by Caren Cameron, Betty Tate, Daphne MacNaughton, Colleen Politano © 1997. May be reproduced for classroom use.

From Building Connections: *Recognition Without Rewards*, by Caren Cameron, Betty Tate, Daphne MacNaughton, Colleen Politano © 1997. May be reproduced for classroom use.

Recognition is:

👆 **authentic:** based on genuine accomplishments that occur every day

👆 **personal:** based on participation and choices of students

👆 **inclusive:** available to all students without condition

👆 **varied:** provides infinite opportunities for recognizing students' successes

SUGGESTED READING

Armstrong, T. 1994. *Multiple intelligences in the classroom.* Alexandria, VA: Association for Supervision and Curriculum Development.

Borba, M. 1994. *Esteem builders resources.* Torrance, CA: Jalmar Press.

Caine, R. N., and Caine, G. 1994. *Making connections: Teaching and the human brain.* Boston: Addison-Wesley.

Costa, A. 1991. *The school as a home for the mind.* Palatine, Illinois: Skylight Publishing.

Gardner, H. 1993. *Multiple intelligences: The theory in practice.* New York: Basic Books.

Goleman et al. 1992. *The creative spirit.* New York: Dutton.

Jensen, E. 1994. *The learning brain.* San Diego, CA: Turning Point Publishing.

———. 1995. *Brain-based learning and teaching.* San Diego, CA: Turning Point Publishing.

Kohn, A. 1986. *No contest: The case against competition.* Boston: Houghton Mifflin.

———. 1991. "Caring kids: The role of the schools." *Phi Delta Kappan* (March): 496–506.

———. 1993. *Punished by rewards: The trouble with gold stars, incentive plans, A's, praise and other bribes.* New York: Houghton Mifflin.

———. 1993. "Rewards versus learning: A response to Paul Chance." *Phi Delta Kappan* 74 (10): 783–787.

Raffini, J. 1993. *Winners without losers: Structures and strategies for increasing student motivation to learn.* Boston: Allyn and Bacon.

Schaps, E., and Lewis, C. 1991. "Extrinsic rewards are education's past, not its future." *Educational Leadership* 48 (7): 81.

Smith, F. 1986. *Insult to intelligence.* New York: Arbour House.

———. 1990. *To think.* New York and London: Teachers College Press.

White, R., and Gunstone, R. 1992. *Probing understanding.* London: The Falmer Press.

REFERENCES

The references that follow are intended to provide the sources cited within the text and to reflect some of the publications that influenced our thinking since the days when we first began to discuss our discomfort with rewards.

Readers may wonder about the fact that our sources do not always deal with the issues of awards and rewards directly. As we conducted searches of the research and literature, we found little that specifically addressed rewards. However, we consistently found information that related to self-esteem, motivation, the processes of learning, and our ideas about the importance of recognition. While some of the references are pre-1990, or may no longer be easily accessible, they provide a history, or record, of the sources we used:

- ☞ Some of our earliest references came out of a movement in the seventies, when coaches and physical educators began to express their discomfort with the negative effects of organized sports and high-level competition for young children. We shared their concerns and applied what they were learning to our own classroom and school contexts.

- ☞ We were influenced by people concerned with the effects of educational practices on the development of both negative and positive self-esteem. The practitioners and researchers who wrote about success and failure in school, cooperative learning, and motivation informed our conversations.

- ☞ We were influenced also by growing bodies of knowledge about the processes of learning. Information about constructivist learning theory, multiple intelligences, the conditions for learning, and brain-based teaching contributed to our commitment to an increasing awareness of the need for change.

- ☞ During the course of individual study and group conversations, we were often struck by publications that addressed changing times and views of education. We became increasingly aware that, while educational practices such as awards and rewards may have served a purpose at one time, these same practices no longer seemed useful or wise.

Amabile, T. 1989. Cited in *The learning brain,* by Eric Jensen. 1994. San Diego, CA: Turning Point Publishing.

Armstrong, T. 1994. *Multiple intelligences in the classroom.* Alexandria, VA: Association for Supervision and Curriculum Development.

Barth, Roland. 1991. *Improving schools from within.* San Francisco: Jossey-Bass.

Beane, J. A., and Lipka, R. P. 1987. *When kids come first: Enhancing self esteem.* Columbus, OH: National Middle School Association.

Borba, M. 1993. *Staff esteem builders.* Torrance, CA: Jalmar Press.

———. 1994. *Esteem builders resources.* Torrance, CA: Jalmar Press.

Brophy, J. 1987. "Synthesis of research on strategies for motivating students to learn." *Educational Leadership* 45 (2): 40–48.

Caine, R. N., and Caine, G. 1994. *Making connections: Teaching and the human brain.* Boston: Addison-Wesley.

Canfield, J. 1987. *Self-esteem in the classroom: A curriculum guide.* Pacific Palisades, CA: Self-Esteem Seminars.

Costa, A. 1991. *The school as a home for the mind.* Palatine, Illinois: Skylight Publishing.

Deci, E. 1978. "Application of research on the effects of rewards." *The hidden costs of rewards: New perspectives on the psychology of human motivation.* Lepper and Greene, editors. Hillsdale, NJ: Lawrence Erlbaum and Associates.

Deci, E., and Ryan, R. M. 1985. *Intrinsic motivation and self-determination in human behavior.* New York: Plenum.

Deci, E. et al. 1991. "Motivation and education: The self-determination perspective." *Educational Psychologist* 26: 325–346.

Eisner, E. W. 1979. *The educational imagination.* New York: Macmillan.

Elkind, D. 1987. "Super kids and super problems." *Psychology Today* (May): 60–61.

Fisk, E. B. 1992. *Smart schools, smart kids.* New York: Simon and Schuster.

Gardner, H. 1983. *Frames of mind: The theory of multiple intelligences.* Tenth anniversary edition. New York: Basic Books.

———. 1993. *Multiple intelligences: The theory in practice.* New York: Basic Books.

Glasser, W. 1990. *The quality school.* New York: Harper and Row.

———. 1986. *Control theory in the classroom.* New York: Harper and Row.

Goble, N. M. 1989. "Schools for the future: New challenges to the agenda of education." Address to Delta School District Conference, November 17, 1989.

Goleman et al. 1992. *The creative spirit.* New York: Dutton.

Greig, S. et al. 1989. *Greenprints for changing schools.* London: The World Wide Fund for Nature and Kogan Page.

Jensen, E. 1994. *The learning brain.* San Diego, CA: Turning Point Publishing.

———. 1995. *Brain-based learning and teaching.* San Diego, CA: Turning Point Publishing.

Kazden, A. 1994. Cited in *The learning brain,* by Eric Jensen. San Diego, CA: Turning Point Publishing.

Kohn, A. 1986a. *No contest: The case against competition.* Boston: Houghton Mifflin.

———. 1986b. "How to succeed without even vying." *Psychology Today* (September):22–28.

———. 1987. "Art for art's sake." *Psychology Today* (September): 52–57.

———. 1987. "It's hard to get left out of a pair." *Psychology Today* (October): 53–57.

———. 1991. "Caring kids: The role of the schools." *Phi Delta Kappan* (March): 496–506.

———. 1993a. *Punished by rewards: The trouble with gold stars, incentive plans, A's, praise and other bribes.* New York: Houghton Mifflin.

———. 1993b. "Rewards versus learning: A response to Paul Chance." *Phi Delta Kappan* 74 (10), 783–787.

Ledell, M., and Arnsparger, A. 1993. *How to deal with community criticism of school change.* Alexandria, VA: Association for Supervision and Curriculum Development, in cooperation with American Association of School Administrators and National Association of State Boards of Education.

Lepper, M. R. 1988. "Motivational considerations in the study of instruction." *Cognition and Instruction* 5 (4): 289–309.

Lepper, M. R., and Cordova, D. I. 1992. "A desire to be taught: Instructional consequences of intrinsic motivation." *Motivation and Emotion* 16: 187–208.

Lumsden, L. S. 1994. "Student motivation to learn." ERIC Digest 92.

Orlick, T. D. 1977. "Against competition." *Reporter* 3 (3).

———. 1978. *The cooperative sports and games book: Challenge without competition.* New York: Pantheon Books.

Orlick, T. D. and Mosher, R. 1978. "Extrinsic awards and participant motivation in a sport-related task." *International Journal of Sport Psychology* 9: 27–39.

Price, R. 1993. "Awards, rewards, and positive reinforcement for students." *The Canadian School Executive* 13 (6): 28–30.

Purkey, W. W. 1970. *Self-concept and school achievement.* Englewood Cliffs, NJ: Prentice-Hall.

———. 1978. *Inviting school success: A self-concept approach to teaching and learning.* Belmont, CA: Wadsworth Publishing.

Raffini, J. 1993. *Winners without losers: Structures and strategies for increasing student motivation to learn.* Boston: Allyn and Bacon.

Rosenthal, R., and Babad, E. Y. 1985. "Pygmalion in the classroom." *Educational Leadership* (September): 36–39.

Schaps, E., and Lewis, C. 1991. "Extrinsic rewards are education's past, not its future." *Educational Leadership* 48 (7): 81.

Shuttleworth, D. E. 1989. "Public education for the post-industrial age." *The Canadian School Executive* (February): 11–13.

Smith, F. 1986. *Insult to intelligence.* New York: Arbour House.

———. 1990. *To think.* New York and London: Teachers College Press.

Sweet, A. P., and Guthrie, G. T. 1996. "How children's motivations relate to literacy development and instruction." *The Reading Teacher* 49 (8): 660–662.

Wesson, P. 1973. "High level competition and the elementary school-aged child." *Health and Physical Education Council Bulletin* 11 (1).

White, R., and Gunstone, R. 1992. *Probing understanding.* London: The Falmer Press.